On with the Show!

Ron Benson

Lynn Bryan

Kim Newlove

Charolette Player

Liz Stenson

CONSULTANTS

Susan Elliott

Diane Lomond

Ken MacInnis

Elizabeth Parchment

Contents

  Selections with this symbol are available on audio.

  This symbol indicates student writing.

❦ Canadian selections are marked with this symbol.

Sing to the Stars

by Mary Brigid Barrett
Illustrated by Sandra Speidel

Ephram walks sprightly down the street. Head high, he swings his black case back and forth, to and fro.

Girls jump rope as Ephram strides by. They hop, they skip, jump, jumping. Beaded and bowed, their braids fly high. Up and down, up and down. The rope slaps the sidewalk, *plat, plat, plat.*

It's late afternoon. Mr. Washington steps out of his

Laundromat, his dog's harness in one hand, his toolbox in the other. He eases himself into a folding chair. Bending forward, he touches his dog, nose to wet nose. Shiloh licks his chin and cheeks. Chuckling, Mr. Washington wipes his face with a big plaid handkerchief. His hand pat, pat, pats his dog and his foot tap, tap, taps the cracked cement.

"How are you today, Ephram?"

Ephram stops. "Evening to you, Mr. Washington," he says, thumping his case against his leg. "Hello there, Shiloh." He pauses. "Mr. Washington, sir, how do you always know it's me walking by?"

"Well, son, every walk's got a rhythm. My ears tell me light step, brush, light step, brush, must be Ephram walking home from his violin lesson, stepping glad and swinging his violin case."

"You can tell I'm happy by the sound of my walk?" asks Ephram.

"Boy, I can tell when your violin teacher has been razzing you and you're full up pitiful with yourself!"

"Really?"

"Oh yes, your shoes clap the cement slow and dull. Your case thuds low against your leg. But that's rare, Ephram. Most times you walk with the song of life in your step. You must make sweet music on that violin. Your grandma says you've got a gift."

"Don't know about that, Mr. Washington," says Ephram. "But I do like to play this violin. It speaks when I haven't got any words. I like to practise after supper, up on the roof."

Mr. Washington smiles broadly. He reaches for Ephram's hand. "Here I thought it was old Mr. Bach, sliding down his 'Jesu, Joy of Man's Desiring' from his heavenly station. And all the time it was you, Ephram, up on that roof."

Ephram pulls his hand away from Mr. Washington. "You heard me on the roof? I thought nobody could hear me out there."

"I keep my apartment windows open in this heat," says Mr. Washington, pointing up toward the windows above the Laundromat. "I heard you playing last night. A breeze swept your music down from the roof, and boy, you play to take my breath away.

"There's a neighborhood concert in the park tomorrow night, a fundraiser for a new playground. It's an open mike. Anyone can play. How 'bout it, Ephram?"

Ephram steps back from Mr. Washington. "A stage and all those people, I—I just don't know," he stammers, clutching his violin case tight against his chest. "I've got to go now, Mr. Washington. Grandma will be keeping supper."

"Goodbye, Ephram." Grabbing Shiloh's harness, Mr. Washington stands. "Remember, Ephram," he calls, "music speaks best when someone listens."

Ephram walks on. Past the rap group on the corner. Past the boom box blaring. Past the glaring neon signs flashing on-off, on-off.

"Hey, man, get yourself an electric guitar!" yells one of the group.

Ephram swings around and fingers his violin case as if he were playing a guitar. Then he slaps the case, spins it, and raises it up onto his shoulder, playing it with an imaginary bow. The rapper flashes him a thumbs-up signal. Smiling, Ephram nods back.

Ephram ducks into his building. Pots and pans clank and clatter through thin walls. Televisions blare. A baby squalls. The air is hot and still in the hallways.

"Grandma, I'm home," says Ephram.

"Hello, Sugar," she says. She wipes the sweat from Ephram's brow and kisses him on top of his head. "Supper's ready. Did you have a fine lesson?"

"Yes. I stopped and talked to Mr. Washington on the way home. I think he knows music, Grandma."

"You bet he knows music, Sugar. Mr. Washington was a professional."

"He was?" says Ephram, sitting down to eat.

"Yes, indeed. Mr. Washington trained as a classical pianist. He was your grandfather's and my neighbor when we were young and living in Harlem. One sweltering summer night we were all invited upstairs to a rent party in our building. Mr. James P. Johnson was there, his hands pounding on the piano keys, one hand playing the rhythms of New Orleans, the other making the keys sing the song of New York. Our music pulsated through the air on that sultry night. From then on Flash Fingers Washington played hot, joyful jazz and cool, soulful blues. You should have heard him play, Ephram," says Grandma. "His fingers flew across the keys. Any piece of music, classical, jazz, old spirituals, he gave it style."

"Grandma, he never told me he could play an instrument. Does he play anymore?"

"Not since he and his little girl were in a car accident. That's when Mr. Washington lost his sight."

"His little girl, Grandma, what happened to his little girl?"

Grandma wraps her arms tight around him. "His little girl died in the accident. I suppose he just lost all his joy. He hasn't played since."

Ephram pushes his plate away. His chair scrapes across the floor as he leaves the table.

"Where are you going?" asks Grandma. "You haven't finished your supper."

Ephram picks up his violin. "I need to practise, Grandma."

Up on the roof, the hubbub bustle of cars and people fades to a murmur. In the twilight, Ephram plays his violin, and its sweet song floats out into the wide night.

The next morning Ephram dresses quickly and runs to the park, his feet beating the sidewalk fast time. The stage is set for the concert. Microphones and amplifiers are tested one, two, three, four. On the stage floor, Ephram sees a piano.

He pauses, then walks on, steady, determined, straight to Mr. Washington's Laundromat.

"You're up early this morning, Ephram."

"I don't have my violin case today, Mr. Washington. How d'you—"

"How did I know it was you? Well, son," says Mr. Washington, unlocking the coin box on the dryer. "I told you before, you've got the song of life in your step. This morning it sounds like you're as bold as Mr. Louis Armstrong's horn laying down the 'Tiger Rag.'"

"Mr. Washington," says Ephram, "I've been thinking about playing at the benefit concert tonight. It'd be an honor to play with Flash Fingers Washington."

"Your grandma told you?"

"Yes, sir."

"Ephram, it's been years since I've played." Placing his hands on a laundry table, Mr. Washington spreads his fingers wide, lifting each one individually, clasping and unclasping his hands. "I don't even know if these hands can make a piano sing anymore, Ephram. And I'm not sure I want to find out."

Ephram slips his hands into Mr. Washington's. "Just come, Mr. Washington. The concert begins at eight o'clock."

At the benefit concert, neighbors greet each other. Parents tap their feet and children clap hands to the music. Ephram sits next to his grandmother, his violin case on his lap. "Do you think Mr. Washington will come, Grandma?" asks Ephram.

"Yes . . . yes, I do believe he'll come," says Grandma. "Save this seat for him, here at the end, so Shiloh can sit right by him."

Ephram looks at his watch, trying to read its face in a beam from the streetlight. "It's too late, Grandma. I told him eight o'clock and it's already past eight-thirty! He would have been here by now."

The group from the corner is rapping on-stage. Their drums fill the air with a pulsating beat. Suddenly, the lights go out. There's a loud thump and a clang from on-stage. "Power outage," someone yells. Metal chairs clink as people rise then sink back into their seats, some chattering, some shouting, all wondering what to do.

"It's this heat," says Grandma. "Too many air conditioners blowing in this town. A brownout, I think they call it."

Ephram takes out his violin. "It's time for me to play now, Grandma."

"Ephram," says Grandma, "how can you play in the dark?"

A wet nose tickles Ephram's elbow, a hand firmly grasps his shoulder. "It's always dark . . . up on the roof, isn't it, Ephram?"

Mr. Washington smiles. "Evening, Rachel," he says. "Shiloh and I couldn't miss your grandson's neighborhood debut. Hope we're not too late."

"It's never too late, Balthazar Washington," says Grandma.

"Mr. Washington, people are beginning to leave. I'm going on-stage to play some of the old songs Grandma sings in church. There's a piano on-stage. Will you play with me, sir?"

Mr. Washington tightens his grip on Shiloh's harness and sits down on the empty chair. He pulls out his handkerchief and wipes the sweat from his face and neck.

"Mr. Washington," says Ephram, "music speaks best when someone listens."

Mr. Washington turns toward Ephram's voice. "Shiloh, you stay here with my friend Rachel. Ephram and ole Flash Fingers Washington, we gonna make some sweet sounds tonight."

Ephram grins widely. "Do you know 'Amazing Grace,' Mr. Washington?"

"Ephram, I was playing 'Amazing Grace' when you were a thought in the good Lord's mind!" Mr. Washington places his hand on Ephram's forearm. "Ready, son?"

"Be careful getting up on that stage, you two," cautions Grandma.

"Don't worry, Grandma," says Ephram. "Mr. Washington sees in the dark."

Up on the stage, Ephram seats Mr. Washington at the piano. The crowd buzzes. Ephram shoulders his violin. He raises his bow and begins "Amazing Grace." Mr. Washington joins in. The hum of the crowd fades, and in the darkness the music sings to the stars.

ABOUT THE AUTHOR   MARY BRIGID BARRETT

Mary Brigid Barrett is a writer, illustrator, and teacher. She likes to spend time with children of all ages, teaching them about the wonders of stories and helping them to be better writers and artists. Mary thinks that she has the best job in the world, because she gets to "write for and work with the best people in the whole world, kids."

Waves and Wings

Illustrated by Frédéric Back

Ayii, Ayii, Ayii

An Inuit Chant

Translated by James Houston

Ayii, ayii, ayii,
My arms, they wave high in the air,
My hands, they flutter behind my back,
They wave above my head
Like the wings of a bird.
Let me move my feet.
Let me dance.
Let me shrug my shoulders.
Let me shake my body.
Let me crouch down.
My arms, let me fold them.
Let me hold my hands under my chin.

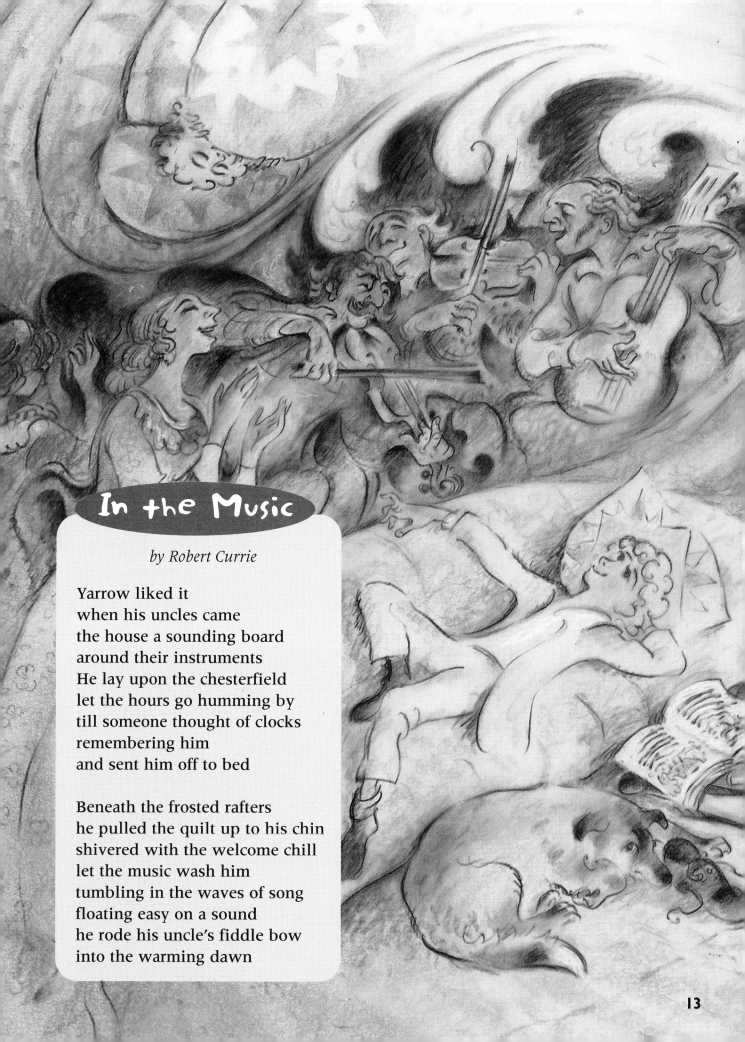

In the Music

by Robert Currie

Yarrow liked it
when his uncles came
the house a sounding board
around their instruments
He lay upon the chesterfield
let the hours go humming by
till someone thought of clocks
remembering him
and sent him off to bed

Beneath the frosted rafters
he pulled the quilt up to his chin
shivered with the welcome chill
let the music wash him
tumbling in the waves of song
floating easy on a sound
he rode his uncle's fiddle bow
into the warming dawn

Powwow

*Written and photographed
by George Ancona*

For a week now, cars, trucks, vans, and trailers have been rolling across the vast, hot prairie. It is time for Crow Fair, the biggest powwow in North America. Every summer, people from all over the United States and Canada travel to the Crow Reservation in Montana to attend Crow Fair. Lakota, Ojibwa, Cheyenne, Crow, Cree, Blackfoot, Fox, and other tribes come from cities, towns, and reservations to celebrate their shared heritage as Native Americans.

One by one, slender wooden poles arc through the air, and their ends are joined together to form the frame of a tepee. The men wrap white canvas around the skeleton, and a new lodge takes its place among the seemingly endless clusters of Crow dwellings. Some of the poles are left with greenery on top to flutter in the breeze.

The powwow is a time for renewing old friendships and making new ones. And it is a time for dancing.

Originally, dances were performed before warriors left the village to hunt, raid, or do battle, and after they returned to celebrate their successes. Other dances were performed as religious ceremonies and to honor individuals or to initiate members of different tribal societies. But not all tribes gathered to dance with others since many were enemies. But nowadays differences are set aside.

Under the shade of the dancing arbor, the drums assemble. At a powwow, a group of singers who sing as they drum a rhythm in unison is called a *drum*.

These singers must know many kinds of songs for all the different dances and special events that take place. The drums become the pulse and heartbeat of the powwow. The master of ceremonies will call upon each of the twenty-eight drums that are attending the fair to take turns singing for the dancers.

Outside the dancing arbor, the dancers gather in a kaleidoscope of feathers, beadwork, fringe, and face paint. Inside the arbor, spectators find seats and wait for the dancing to begin. A feeling of excitement and anticipation fills the air.

The first to dance are the Traditional men. Years ago, Native Americans lived close to nature, and this is reflected in the Traditional dancer's clothes. Feathers from eagles and other birds, porcupine quills, shells, horsehair, and the skins from deer, ermine, otter, wolf, and other animals are worn.

Traditional men wear a single bustle tied to the lower back. Some wear feathered bonnets, while others wear a warrior's hairpiece, called a roach, made from deer tail, porcupine, or horsehair with one or two feathers in the centre.

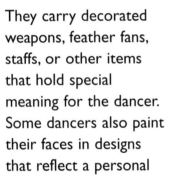

They carry decorated weapons, feather fans, staffs, or other items that hold special meaning for the dancer. Some dancers also paint their faces in designs that reflect a personal vision. These designs can come from a dream or an important experience the dancer has had.

The Native Americans who lived on the Plains survived by hunting. The animals' flesh was used for food, skins became clothing, sinew became thread for sewing, and antlers and bones were made into tools. It was believed that the only way animals could be hunted and killed was if they understood the hunter's need and willingly gave themselves up to him. And if their gift of life was not respected, the next time the hunter went out, the animals would hide. Because of this relationship and dependence on nature, dancers honor the spirits of the animals whose bodies have become part of their dance clothes. They treat these clothes with respect and care.

With the coming of Europeans, new items were introduced to Native Americans through trade. Cloth of cotton or wool, called trade cloth, was made into shirts and leggings. Ribbons appeared, and colorful glass beads replaced dyed porcupine quills for decorating moccasins, vests, and other items. Metal bells were tied to the dancers' legs to accent the rhythm of the drum.

The dance of the Traditional men is dramatic. Some dancers imitate the movements of animals or birds. Others move in a crouched position as if tracking or hunting. The dancers echo a past when men relied on their skills as hunters and warriors to survive.

There is a change in mood when the Traditional women dancers enter the dancing arbor. With their backs straight and heads held high, they move in a regal manner. Each dancer carries a beautiful shawl draped over one arm, and in the opposite hand she holds an eagle-feather fan. Their dance steps have a slight dip that makes the fringe on their clothes sway gently to the rhythm of the drum. The strength and beauty of their movement fills the arbor.

Like those of the Traditional men, the women's clothes reflect a closeness to nature. Dresses are often made from the skins of animals such as deer and elk and are decorated with porcupine quills, cowrie shells, and elk teeth. But the influence of trade with Europeans can also be seen. Cotton and wool trade cloth can be used for dresses. Machine-made fringe decorates shawls, and glass beads glint from dress yokes, sleeves, moccasins, and leggings.

Next come the Fancy dancers. The men are the first to perform. What makes them stand out from the Traditional dancers is color—lots and lots of vibrant color. Equally beautiful are the Fancy women dancers. They wear their shawls over their shoulders while holding the ends in their hands. At times, the dancers look like exotic birds in flight.

At the end of each dance, the dancers leave the arbor hot, tired, and thirsty. Outside the arbor is a fairway with concession stands selling all kinds of food and drink. The dancers can rest and cool off with a soda pop or ice cream. And it's always fun to share some fry bread or a hot dog with friends.

There are also stands where dancers can buy materials for their dance clothes. Skins, feathers, beads, bells, shawls, and many other items are for sale. Tape recordings of the different drums, T-shirts, and other souvenirs can also be found along the fairway.

Back in the dancing arbor, a new drum is selected, and as the singers' voices fill the air, the Grass dancers begin to weave and bend to the music. This is a man's dance based on old war-society dances of the northern plains. In this fast-stepping style, the dancer almost appears to be falling off balance, then catching himself just in time.

In contrast to the fast-paced, teetering style of the Grass dancers is the gentle grace of the Jingle-dress dancers.

The Jingle-dress dance is very old. Originally, each dancer's dress had a shell hanging from it for every day of the year. Today, instead of shells, the tin tops from small cans are rolled into cones and sewn on the dress. During the dance, the cones strike one another, producing a pleasant tinkling sound.

Children of all ages participate at powwows, learning about their heritage. And just like the adults, they can compete for prizes in the different dance categories. Even the youngest, the tiny tots, have a special place of their own at the powwow. They would not miss the fun of the powwow for anything in the world.

ABOUT THE

AUTHOR GEORGE ANCONA

George Ancona is an award-winning author-photographer who has created more than seventy books for children. His books have received many honors, including the New York Times Best Illustrated Picture Book of the Year Award, a New York Academy of Science Award, and the Texas Bluebonnet Award. George currently lives in Santa Fe, New Mexico.

Make Music!

by Eric Nagler and Diana Buckley
Illustrated by Joe Weissmann

Some people are discouraged to find they can't keep a beat. I believe each of us is born with "natural" rhythm but it often gets trained out of us as we grow up.

As we grow up we're taught to use our heads and solve problems rationally . . . to place controls on our bodies and feelings. Unfortunately, heads aren't very good at rhythm. Music and rhythm are expressions of the whole body acting in regular motion, and when our mind tries to be the leader, rhythm breaks down. If you want to rediscover your natural rhythm, ask your head to take a back seat and let your body lead the way.

The Plastic Bottle Calabash

To make a calabash, you need two 2.5 cm rings (macramé rings from a craft store work well), one plastic shampoo bottle, an assortment of beads, nylon cord or wire, scissors, and duct tape.

Cut eight lengths of string, each about one and a half times the height of the bottle in length, and tie them to the ring as in the diagram. Use tape to keep the ring centred to the bottom of the bottle.

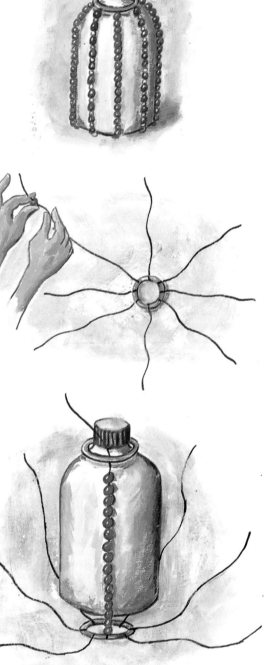

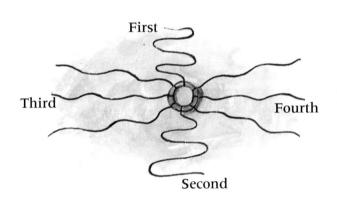

String the beads and tie the strings to the top ring. Trim off the excess string, remove the tape, and "voilà"!

The calabash is a little easier to play if you push a dowel through the mouth of the bottle to make a handle. Secure the dowel with duct tape.

The calabash can be shaken, hit against your hand, or tossed and caught in rhythm to music.

Pop Bottle Whistles

You may know that if you blow across the mouth of a pop bottle you can get a note. Position the lip of the bottle just under your lower lip, pucker slightly, and blow a jet of air across and into the bottle. The pitch of the note has to do with the ratio of pop in your tummy and pop left in the bottle.

This one definitely works. My friend Joe Hampson can play tunes with a pop bottle that has had about one large gulp removed. By changing the shape of his lips and tilting the bottle, he can play an entire scale of notes.

The Spoons

The spoons are one of my favorites. They're accessible and easy to play and get good at. But spoons can be very loud and percussive, so be attentive. If the people around you are holding their ears and making gruesome faces, you may be playing too loudly.

I use a matching pair of round soup spoons . . . NOT MY MOM'S BEST SILVER. Crummy spoons usually sound better anyway. Smaller spoons work better for smaller hands.

Test out several until you get a pair that sound good to you. I put duct tape on the inside of the bowls of my spoons so they make a "clunk" rather than a "clank." I also tape the ends of each spoon so they are less likely to fly out of my hand. I don't tape the spoons together, though. Spoons attached at the ends of the handles can't be used in different ways. I do put tape on the handle of the bottom spoon–the one that goes between my first and second fingers–so that the metal doesn't dig into my skin. I also bend the top and bottom spoons differently so they fit my hand comfortably and the bowls strike in the centre.

To play the spoons, put them back-to-back and grab the handles with your index finger in between, separating the bowls as in the picture. **Hold them rather tightly so they don't flop around.** Hit your knee with the spoons so that the top one bangs against the bottom one. When you have a good rhythm and the spoons are not flopping all over the place, try holding your other hand above them and hit it on the upswing. Hitting your upper hand every other time gives a basic "Lone Ranger" rhythm. You know . . . "Where did the Lone Ranger take the garbage?" "To the dump . . . to the dump . . . to the dump, dump, dump."

Advanced spoonists can try the "brush." Spread your fingers out stiff, run the bottom spoon across the fingers and onto your knee. It makes a drum roll effect.

Spoons are great percussion instruments to accompany your own songs. Make up your own "rap" for your own spoon tune.

The Psaltery

The psaltery has a pure and fragile sound that seems very ancient. Each string you pluck rings and rings, coloring all the notes that come after.

The psaltery is a box with strings stretched across it. That makes it a relative of the zither, the autoharp, the harpsichord, and the piano.

To make a successful psaltery it is important to pay attention to the relationship between the string and the box. A cardboard shoe box, for example, is delicate and requires a thin string like a rubber band. A stronger box like a metal cookie container requires a stronger string, like a metal banjo string. Remember that some materials vibrate better than others. A flat wooden box (if you can find one) vibrates better than a cardboard one.

The string must make contact with the box in such a way as to vibrate the soundboard. Two bridges made of small lengths of wood help do this. Glue them across the box at each end and run the strings over them.

The strings should be tunable. That is, they should be attached to something that turns.

Sometimes, it's a good idea to reinforce the box where the tuners are attached, so it can withstand the tension of the strings.

The diagram shows a simple psaltery made from nylon guitar strings or fishing line. The box is a wooden box (use cardboard if you have to), and the pegs are screw eyes.

Tune your psaltery in *do, re, mi* fashion, and find pleasing note combinations to accompany your song.

The Comb Kazoo

When I invite people up on stage to play with me, the comb kazoo is the instrument that takes the most courage because you don't just blow into it; you have to use your voice to play it.

A kazoo is more like an "amplifier" than an instrument. It uses a little piece of wax paper and a tube to change the sound of your voice and make it a little louder.

You can buy a kazoo in a music store, but don't. It's simple to make your own for free. All it takes is a comb and a piece of wax paper about fifteen centimetres long.

Fold the waxed paper over the comb once. Keep the paper stretched tight. Make an "oooo" sound with your lips and voice. Don't blow! It's your vocal cords that vibrate the air. Bring the kazoo close to your mouth and just touch it to your lips so you can feel it tickle.

Most people hum into their kazoos, but there are many different things to do to make the sound more interesting. Try imitating a horn, going "wah, wah," or even wailing. You can push all sorts of mouth sounds through the kazoo and make some interesting music.

ABOUT THE AUTHOR ERIC NAGLER

Eric Nagler is the star of the television show "Eric's World," and he has released several highly praised records. Live concerts, however, remain Nagler's first love. He explains, "At my concerts, families are encouraged to participate and to share in the joy of making music. Many bring their own instruments to the show . . . together we sing, clap, rattle, and dance our way through the performance."

The Yes Essay

It seems like you sink into another world when you hear this music. Even on the covers of the Yes CDs and cassettes you can find fairy trees and weird crystal towers.

Yes has lots of styles; most of them have something to do with rock music. Some of the songs are not even songs; they just have music in them. That is because Yes music makes a great impression of something fairylike, magical, and beautiful.

Now I will tell you a little bit about the history of Yes. Yes started their career at the end of the sixties. With their first album Yes won great success, so they went on recording more songs. The Yes members often changed but the Yes style itself stayed the same. All of the members kept the same fairylike and magical style.

I am a big fan of Yes. I think Yes is a great group. I say, if you want to hear them all play, you should hear their album *Union*. It will give you an impression of what Yes really is.

My favorite Yes album is *Relayer*. I think it is because I like rock, and *Relayer* has three brilliant rock songs on it.

Ivan Poukhovski
Grade 5

Music

What is music?
Music is rock 'n roll, hip hop, country, and rap.
Music is loud, so you can't hear yourself.
Music is something to be proud of because you listen to it every day.

Music is great,
Music is cool,
and something that we can't live without.
Music is good to have and
to listen to.

THAT'S MUSIC!!!

Beata Laskowska
Age 13

I love writing. I think it has strong power over me. In writing I can present my thoughts and imagination in a fancy way. I think in writing everything is possible!

Ivan Poukhovski

The Dance

My friend, her mom came from France,
She loved to dance,
Only I could prance,
So her mom taught me to dance,
Now I'm moving to France,
                            Au revoir.

Franny Campagna
Grade 6

Moving to the Beat

Once upon a time there lived a boy named Kurt. He was one of the most popular boys in the school. Kurt loved sports, social studies, math, and alternative music. There was one thing that Kurt absolutely hated: band. He couldn't stand watching or listening to bands play.

One day, Kurt's best friend, Danny, begged Kurt to come to watch Danny's band perform. Kurt told Danny that he wouldn't go because he didn't like bands. That night Kurt asked his family if he should go and they all said yes.

So, on the night of the performance, Kurt decided to go. On the schedule it said that the band was going to play four songs. During the second song, Kurt's foot began to fall asleep. He stomped it down about five times to try to wake it up. Then all of a sudden everybody in the room began to stomp because they thought that he was tapping his foot to the beat.

After a while, Mrs. Donvers, the principal, started to dance. Then all you could see were people dancing. As a matter of fact, everybody was having so much fun that for the rest of the night everybody danced until they had to go home.

Gina Middleton
Age 11

Meet Edgar Degas

by Anne Newlands

Self-Portrait in a Soft Hat
1857-58
Oil on paper mounted on canvas
26 x 19 cm
Sterling and Francine Clark Art Institute, Williamstown, Massachusetts

Edgar Degas was luckier than many painters: he was famous during his long lifetime and his work was much in demand. Yet Degas was still a rebel. He feuded with other artists and battled with the art critics. Some were angered because his work was not pretty. Others were insulted because he thought they were fools.

Degas was born more than 150 years ago, before people knew how to record voices, so we don't know exactly what he sounded like. But we do know many things about his character, thanks to letters and notebooks he left behind and other peoples' stories about him. These tell us that he loved to talk and argue about art, politics, and life.

Here we have given Edgar Degas a voice that we hope suits him. Let's meet Edgar Degas and look at his pictures with him.

Dance Class at the Opéra
1872
Oil on canvas
32 x 46 cm
Musée D'Orsay, Paris

Practice Makes Perfect

A critic once said that if you saw my ballet paintings, you didn't have to go to a live performance. It was meant as a compliment, so I didn't want to tell him that he had missed the point. I am fascinated not so much by the dance as by the way the human body moves. For me, the ballet is a good place to study motion.

We are watching a class at the Paris Opéra. Light shines through the large windows outside the picture frame. The dancers look delicate in their crisp, white dresses, but they are really as strong as horses. Their grace comes from hard work, sweat, and pain. The ballerinas around the walls are stretching their legs and feet so their muscles will not stiffen up. But everyone else is still. The dancer in the middle of the room is poised to begin. The violinist waits for the signal to play. At a word from the ballet master in the white suit, the room will come alive.

What a Star!

We are watching the ballet from a box seat at the side of the theatre. From here we can look down at the dancer and also see what's happening beside the stage, in the "wings."

The star is alone on the huge dark stage. She shimmers in the bright light, her outstretched arms forming an elegant curve. She seems to balance effortlessly on one leg. But look closely. Could this leg really support her? Perhaps not, but that didn't matter to me as much as showing how light and shadow can make a figure seem to move.

The other dancers are off-stage, waiting behind the scenery and watching the magic of the dance. A man dressed in black—perhaps a friend of the star—also watches from the wings.

The Star
1876-77
Pastel over monotype
58 x 42 cm
Musée D'Orsay, Paris

The Fourteen-Year-Old Dancer

This is Marie van Goethem, a fourteen-year-old dance student at the Paris Opéra. She is not unusual—neither pretty nor very talented. But because I chose her as a model for my sculpture, she is now famous.

I made my sculpture out of wax, which I tinted a flesh color. I bought a wig at a puppet store and tied it up with a ribbon. I dressed her in a real ballet costume and silk slippers and covered everything but the skirt with wax. And there she stands, holding her head proudly!

When my sculpture was first exhibited, people were uncomfortable looking at her. But they couldn't tear themselves away. They were fascinated because she looked so lifelike, all dressed and almost two-thirds her natural size. They expected to see a beautiful ballet dancer. But Marie is just herself—skinny, small, and homely.

My sculpture caused an uproar! People were furious, and I was delighted!

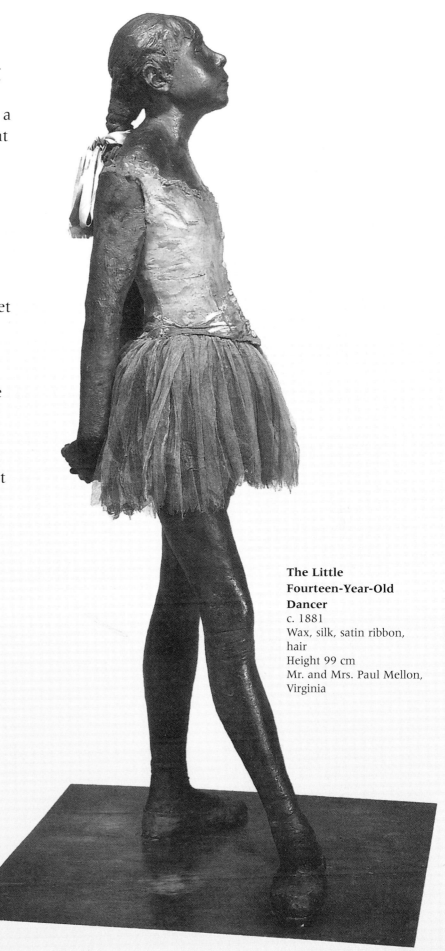

The Little Fourteen-Year-Old Dancer
c. 1881
Wax, silk, satin ribbon, hair
Height 99 cm
Mr. and Mrs. Paul Mellon, Virginia

Dancers, Pink and Green
c. 1890
Oil on canvas
82.2 x 75.6 cm
The Metropolitan Museum of Art, New York
Bequest of Mrs. H.O. Havemeyer 1929, The H.O. Havemeyer Collection

A Moving Picture

You may think this is a group of dancers before they go on stage, but look more closely, for I am very cunning. It is not a group—I made this picture up from sketches and drawings of one dancer in several poses. I created a setting for the poses by adding stage scenery, extra figures in the background, and the silhouette of a man.

When I put the sketches together, my dancer appears to move. First she faces us: her head is down and her hands are on her hips. Then she turns her back to us and leans into the stage set. As she walks around it she raises her head and moves her arms, first to her shoulder and then higher, to fix her hair. At any moment, she could step on stage and dance.

Falling Star

by Vivien Alcock
Illustrated by Anne Villeneuve

I was so happy. I wanted to dance in the wet streets, singing, "They've chosen me! They've chosen me!"

But my brother would have said I was showing off. Ted is always cross when Mom gets him to fetch me home from my ballet class on Tuesdays. It's not my fault she won't let me walk home alone, not in winter when it's dark early.

Ted hates ballet, anyway. When Mom took us to see *Swan Lake* three years ago, he grumbled and fidgeted, picked his nose and kicked the seat in front of him, until the lady turned round and complained. Mom said she was ashamed of him. I hadn't even noticed.

My eyes were dazzled. I saw nothing but the dancers leaping and spinning, caught like butterflies in a golden net of light.

When it was over, I didn't clap. I just sat there, staring.

"What's the matter, Liz?" Mom asked. "You look terribly pale. I hope you're not sickening for something."

"I'm going to be a ballerina when I grow up," I said.

My mind was quite made up. All I wanted to do was dance. Now and for ever.

It was a pity I didn't seem to be very good at it. Mom enrolled me at the Pelling School of Dance and Drama, Tuesdays and Thursdays after school. Everyone there was better than me, except poor Pam Greene, who's hopeless. Her legs are too short and fat; mine are too long and thin. They got tangled up in the little running steps. I kept stumbling. Once I fell right over, crash bang on the floor. Everyone laughed.

"You're not hurt, are you, dear?" Miss Isobel Pelling said, helping me up. "Try not to get so excited. Don't throw your legs about so wildly. This isn't a football match."

I hated her.

Then she said something I couldn't hear to Mrs. Woods, who plays the piano. Mrs. Woods sighed and shook her head. I hated her too. I just knew they were saying I would never be any good, and should they tell my mother not to waste her money. I wanted to cry.

But that was last term. Tonight I loved them both. I loved the whole world. I even loved Ted . . . I looked at him sideways. Should I tell him? He wouldn't be interested . . . But I was so excited, I had to tell someone.

"They've chosen me! *Me!*" I said, doing a little *pas seul* round a puddle. "I'm to be in the Christmas ballet!"

"You were in it last year," he complained. "I was there, remember? Mom made me come. You were a snowball—"

"A snow fairy," I said coldly.

He's a beast, I thought. Always making fun of me, just because I'm younger. Why should I care what he thinks, the brainless slob? Except that he's the only brother I've got, and I can't help wishing that once, just once, he'd be proud of me.

"That wasn't the proper Christmas ballet," I told him. "That's just something the school puts on each year for the moms and dads to watch. Only the babies and the juniors who haven't been chosen for the ballet take part. This is quite different. It's the senior show. They only take six of us from the juniors. Miss Pelling says it's a great honor to be chosen."

I didn't tell him there were only seven in the junior class this year, and I was the last they'd picked. Even then, they'd hesitated between me and Pam Greene, who dances like an elephant with five left feet. She didn't cry when she was left out. She gave me a wobbly smile and said, "Well done, Liz." It made me feel *awful*, because I couldn't help feeling happy, too. I thought she was very brave. But that's show business, I suppose. You have to take the rough with the smooth.

"It's going to be in the town hall," I told Ted. "On the

proper stage where they have the pantomimes. And somebody's coming from the *Hornsey Journal* to take photographs."

"Big deal," he said, yawning. "And what are you going to be this time?"

"A star," I mumbled.

"What?" He stared at me in surprise. He was impressed at last. "Really, Liz? Well done! You must be good. Who'd have thought it! My sister is already a star."

It wasn't a lie. I *was* going to be a star. All six of us juniors were going to be stars, only not the sort he imagined. We were to be twinkle, twinkle little stars in silver tutus, dancing around a ballerina moon against a dark-blue canvas sky. Right at the back of the stage, that's where we were going to be, on a raised platform painted to look like rooftops.

In front of us, seven seniors in furry leotards, with painted whiskery faces and big pointed ears fixed to their heads, were to dance to a tune from *Cats*, while half-hidden in the background, we skipped round the ballerina moon.

"Skip, I said, not trip, Liz," Miss Pelling told me, as we rehearsed. "Do try and concentrate on what you're doing. Keep within those chalk marks, that's the size the platform will be. We can't have you falling down among the cats."

She made me nervous. I had enough to worry about already. Ted still thought I was going to be one of the ballerinas, as if I could be at my age. I'm not even allowed to dance on my *pointes* yet, in case I damage my toes while my bones are still bendy. Ted doesn't know anything about ballet.

Mom does. She made my costume, all silver net and sequins, with a painted headdress with five shining points. I asked her not to tell Ted I was only going to be a cardboard and tinsel star, one of six, because I knew he'd laugh himself sick.

"But, darling, he'll find out. He's coming with us—"

"Tell him he can't!"

"Liz, how can I? He offered to come off his own bat. I didn't even have to hint. Besides, it's a great thing to have been chosen to be in the senior ballet."

"Ted won't think so. He'll think it's funny. He'll call me Twinkle-Toes or something sick-making for the rest of my life. I wish they'd chosen Pam Greene and not me! I really do!"

Yet sometimes it was fun. At the dress rehearsal, with everyone in costume: the cats, us stars, and the shining ballerina moon, with the spotlights falling down on us like golden streamers—then all the magic came back. It was fairyland again and I was part of it.

"Isn't it wonderful!" I said to Miss Pelling, when we were all changing to go home.

She smiled rather anxiously. "Don't get over-excited tomorrow, Liz," she said. "We don't want you falling over, do we?"

She shouldn't have said that. I kept thinking of it when we waited in the wings the next night, exchanging nervous smiles. Stomachs somersaulting . . . legs turning to limp string . . . wanting to be sick . . .

The music began. The curtain rose. There we were dancing round the pirouetting moon, while the cats leaped and whirled below us.

I swear it wasn't my fault. Somebody's foot caught my ankle, and I went flying. I missed the ballerina moon by a millimetre, shot off the edge of our platform, and landed on the stage below. My feet skidded wildly on the boards.

I mustn't fall down! *I mustn't!* Miss Pelling would never forgive me. Ted would never stop laughing at me. Mom would be ashamed.

I waved my arms like a windmill, trying to keep my balance. Round and round I tottered, swerving to avoid crashing into the leaping cats. I was getting giddy. I grabbed

at a rope: it turned out to be a tabby tail. It came off in my hand. The cat it belonged to, now a Manx, hissed at me and pushed me towards the wings. I hit the curtains and subsided gently on to the floor. The dusty velvet billowed out and hid me from the roaring audience.

Somebody pulled me farther back into the wings. It was Miss Pelling. "Never mind, Liz," she sighed. "You're not hurt, are you?"

"No."

But I was hurt. I was shamed, my future career was in ruins. Never would I dance again, never! I wished I were dead.

Mr. Dawson from Drama tiptoed over and crouched down beside me.

"Brilliant," he whispered, patting my shoulder and beaming at me. "Absolutely brilliant. Why aren't you in my drama class? You're a born clown."

I didn't want to be in a circus, having buckets of water thrown at me. I wanted to be on a stage, having bouquets of flowers. Yet he seemed so pleased with me, as if I'd done something clever.

The audience was pleased with me too. When the show was over, and the dancers took their bows, they shouted for me. "Where's the falling star?" Somebody pushed me forward and everyone cheered. I could see Ted clapping like mad and Mom smiling. I couldn't understand it.

"They thought it was intentional," Miss Pelling explained to me later. "They thought you were *meant* to be a shooting star. I wonder if we should keep it in . . . No, no, too risky, I'm afraid. Pity. It really was very funny."

"I could easily do it again," I offered. "I'm going to be a comedienne when I grow up. I thought I'd change over to Drama next term. And I might take singing lessons so I can be in musical comedy."

"That's a splendid idea, Liz," she said, thankfully.

ABOUT THE

AUTHOR VIVIEN ALCOCK

Vivien Alcock started writing when she was just a young child. She found that writing helped her to deal with difficult times in her life, such as her parents' divorce and her mother's serious illness. However, Vivien did not become a professional writer until she was older and was the mother of a young daughter herself. Then, it was her daughter's love of being told stories that made Vivien decide to start writing again. Vivien has now had over ten books published, including *The Mysterious Mr. Ross* and *The Trial of Anna Cotman*.

An Interview with Bing-Go the Clown

by Beverley Kula

Jim Price, alias Bing-Go the Clown, lives in Sherwood Park, Alberta. He has been performing as a clown for many hospitals and charities for the past eleven years. Bing-Go also performs professionally for school groups, businesses, parties, and special celebrations. He stands out in a crowd because of his big blue hair, big shoes, and big voice!

Why did you choose clowning as a profession?

Clowning is a very easy way to become an actor and to play a role. It is a role that brings pleasure to everyone around you. Clowning makes people happy, and I like being able to make people laugh.

What different kinds of clowns are there, and how did you choose which kind of clown to be?

In North America, there are three types of clowns—the White Face Clown, the Aguste Clown, and the Tramp Clown. The White Face is always the happy clown. The Aguste Clown has a multi-colored face and mismatched clothes. He's always the butt of other clowns' jokes. The Tramp Clown is the hard-times clown, the one everyone feels sorry for. In clown history, Emmett Kelley and Lou Jacobson were famous Tramp Clowns, but perhaps the most famous of all was Red Skelton.

I chose to be a White Face Clown because children like this kind of clown. Maybe that's because the White Face Clown is always happy and friendly, and he's also the "birthday clown."

Why do you call yourself Bing-Go?

Every clown picks a name. I wanted a name that would be easy to say and remember. "Bingo" is a word everybody knows. I spelled my name differently from the title of the game so people would remember it. Sometimes children on the street yell, "Hey, there goes Bing-Go!" even when they haven't seen me for a couple of years. So I guess the name works!

Does Bing-Go always look the same? How long does it take to get ready for a performance?

Professional clowns develop a certain look and character. Famous clowns even register their faces at the Clown Hall of Fame in Wisconsin. Then no other clown can paint the same kind of face.

Bing-Go has blue hair, a simple white face, and a brightly colored costume.

Over the years, I've tried to create a face that would be attractive to children and not scary. I wear a half-wig instead of a full wig because I'm tall and a full wig might make me look huge to a small child. Bing-Go always looks the same—he doesn't change. He does have a summer costume and a winter costume, though.

When I first started, it took me about an hour and fifteen minutes to get my

◀ A Tramp Clown.

make-up and costume on. Now I can be dressed and out the door in less than fifteen minutes!

Bing-Go wears enormous shoes. Are your feet really that big?

They feel that big! I had Bing-Go's shoes specially made by a shoemaker. He took a pair of my normal shoes and built clown shoes on top.

How did you decide how Bing-Go would act?

I wanted to be a happy, funny clown, but it still took training and experience to develop the character of Bing-Go. He's eight years old, and he will always be eight years old. He doesn't have to behave like an adult. He can get things mixed up as a younger child might do. He may misunderstand what the audience has said, or reach the wrong conclusion about what he has been told. He is a bit silly and confused, and at times he doesn't listen very well!

How long have you been a clown? How did you get started?

I started clowning eleven years ago. I began with the Shriners organization. I joined the Shriners' clown corps and I really liked it. I decided that I should do it right, so I started to learn how to become a professional clown.

What kind of clown training did you get?

You have to go to school to learn all about clowning. The most famous school in North America is the Ringling Brothers Clown School in Florida. I didn't try to go there because I thought I was too old to train as a circus clown.

Another well-known clown school is at the University of Wisconsin. The school offers a clown camp for six weeks every year. I attended the camp in Wisconsin, and also when it came to Edmonton, Alberta, and to Medicine Hat, Alberta. I've attended study sessions put

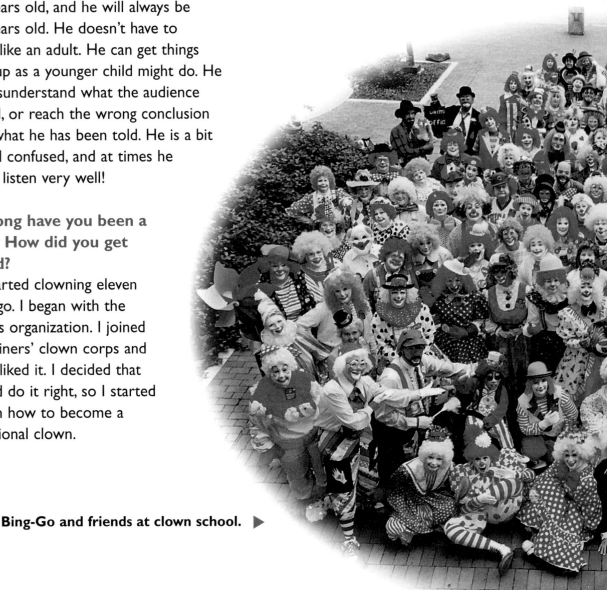

Bing-Go and friends at clown school. ▶

on by the World Clown Association, and International Clowns of America seminars, too.

Is clown school different from other kinds of school? What do you learn there?

Picture a group of about one hundred and twenty men, women, boys, and girls, all dressed up in different clown costumes, with full make-up, taking classes! Clowns learn how to act and how to develop character. Applying make-up, making balloon animals, developing skits, and performing basic magic are all part of the training. Clowns also learn how to work with different groups of people, such as children, sick people, or seniors' groups. The teachers and clowns perform for each other and share ideas and skills. There is lots of laughter and lots of noise. Clown school is never dull!

Bing-Go, you include magic as part of your performance. Do most clowns do magic? Why did you choose to do magic?

No, most clowns do not do magic. I chose magic because of my first clowning experiences as a Shrine Clown visiting sick children in the hospital. I noticed that when the clowns visited the children's ward of the hospital, each clown could entertain one child at a time, but then the rest of the children would be waiting for their turn. I thought that it would be nice if I could entertain thirty children all at once. I decided to learn some small hand magic—not the big magic that the famous magicians do on TV, but simpler tricks. I developed a routine of magic tricks, which I have added to over the years. I now do a stage show where I do not do the magic— the children do. The children are holding the hat when the napkin changes into a dove, or the bowl when the rubber fish become live goldfish. Of course Bing-Go gets pretty confused with the magic, so he needs lots of help from the audience!

Where do you like performing best?

Circus performances are exciting because there are more clowns and bigger props. You really hear a roar when people laugh! I enjoy my smaller performances even more, though. At birthday parties or schools the crowd is very involved in what I do, especially when I do magic tricks. I love seeing the looks on their faces when something magical happens.

Do you get paid for your performances?

Sometimes I perform as a member of the Edmonton Shriners' Clown Unit. I don't get paid for those performances. I do get paid for performing at birthday parties or at special celebrations put on by a city, business, or school.

What is your most memorable experience as a clown?

The second year that I was clowning, I was doing a show at a hospital. There was a little girl lying on her stomach on a hospital bed. She had had a back operation that day, and she was in a lot of pain. She was crying. I asked her mother if we could wheel her down the hallway because we were going to do a show. We included her in the show, and she actually stopped crying and started laughing. At the end of the show her mother came up and thanked me. She said, "You made her forget her pain for a little while." That is one moment I will never forget.

Mirette on the High Wire

Written and illustrated by Emily Arnold McCully

One hundred years ago in Paris, when theatres and music halls drew travelling players from all over the world, the best place to stay was at the widow Gâteau's, a boarding house on English Street.

Acrobats, jugglers, actors, and mimes from as far away as Moscow and New York reclined on the widow's feather mattresses and devoured her kidney stews.

Madame Gâteau worked hard to make her guests comfortable, and so did her daughter, Mirette. The girl was an expert at washing linens, chopping leeks, paring potatoes, and mopping floors. She was a good listener too. Nothing pleased her more than to overhear the vagabond players tell of their adventures in this town and that along the road.

One evening a tall, sad-faced stranger arrived. He told Madame Gâteau he was Bellini, a retired high-wire walker.

"I am here for a rest," he said.

"I have just the room for you, Monsieur Bellini: in the back, where it's quiet," she said. "But it's on the ground floor, with no view."

"Perfect," said the stranger. "I will take my meals alone."

The next afternoon, when Mirette came for the sheets, there was the stranger, crossing the courtyard on air! Mirette was enchanted. Of all the things a person could do, this must be the most magical. Her feet tingled, as if they wanted to jump up on the wire beside Bellini.

Mirette worked up the courage to speak. "Excuse me, Monsieur Bellini, I want to learn to do that!" she cried.

Bellini sighed. "That would not be a good idea," he said. "Once you start, your feet are never happy again on the ground."

"Oh, please teach me!" Mirette begged. "My feet are already unhappy on the ground." But he shook his head.

Mirette watched him every day. He would slide his feet onto the wire, cast his eyes ahead, and cross without ever looking down, as if in a trance.

Finally she couldn't resist any longer. When Bellini was gone, she jumped up on the wire to try it herself. Her arms flailed like windmills. In a moment she was back on the ground. Bellini made it look so easy. Surely she could do it too if she kept trying.

In ten tries she balanced on one foot for a few seconds. In a day, she managed three steps without wavering. Finally, after a week of many, many falls, she walked the length of the wire. She couldn't wait to show Bellini.

He was silent for a long time. Then he said, "In the beginning everyone falls. Most give up. But you kept trying. Perhaps you have talent as well."

"Oh, thank you," said Mirette.

She got up two hours earlier every day to finish her chores before the sun shone in the courtyard. The rest of the day was for lessons and practice.

Bellini was a strict master. "Never let your eyes stray," he told her day after day. "Think only of the wire, and of crossing to the end."

When she could cross dozens of times without falling, he taught her the wire-walker's salute. Then she learned to run, to lie down, and to turn a somersault.

"I will never ever fall again!" Mirette shouted.

"Do not boast," Bellini said, so sharply that Mirette lost her balance and had to jump down.

One night an agent from Astley's Hippodrome in London rented a room. He noticed Bellini on his way to dinner.

"What a shock to see him here!" he exclaimed.

"See who?" asked a mime.

"Why, the great Bellini! Didn't you know he was in the room at the back?"

"Bellini . . . the one who crossed Niagara Falls on a three-hundred-metre wire in ten minutes?" asked the mime.

"And on the way back stopped in the middle to cook an omelette on a stove full of live coals. Then he opened a bottle of champagne and toasted the crowd," the agent recalled.

"My uncle used to talk about that," said a juggler.

"Bellini crossed the Alps with baskets tied to his feet, fired a cannon over the bull ring in Barcelona, walked a flaming wire wearing a blindfold in Naples—the man had the nerves of an iceberg," the agent said.

Mirette raced to Bellini's room.

"Is it true?" she cried. "You did all those things? Why didn't you tell me? I want to do them too! I want to go with you!"

"I can't take you," said Bellini.

"But why not?" asked Mirette.

Bellini hesitated a long time. "Because I am afraid," he said at last.

Mirette was astonished. *"Afraid?"* she said. "But *why?*"

"Once you have fear on the wire, it never leaves," Bellini said.

"But you must *make* it leave!" Mirette insisted.

"I cannot," said Bellini.

Mirette turned and ran to the kitchen as tears sprang to her eyes. She had felt such joy on the wire. Now Bellini's fear was like a cloud casting its black shadow on all she had learned from him.

Bellini paced his room for hours. It was terrible to disappoint Mirette! By dawn he knew that if he didn't face his fear at last, he could not face Mirette. He knew what he must do. The question was, could he succeed?

That night, when the agent returned, Bellini was waiting for him. The agent listened to Bellini's plan with mounting excitement. "I'll take care of it," he promised. To himself he added, "A big crowd will make me a tidy profit. What luck I just happened to be in Paris now."

Bellini went out to find a length of hemp with a steel core. He borrowed a winch and worked until daylight securing the wire.

The next evening, Mirette heard the commotion in the street.

"Go and see what it is," her mother said. "Maybe it will cheer you up."

In the square was a hubbub. The crowd was so thick she couldn't see, at first, that the agent was aiming a spotlight at the sky.

". . . return of the great Bellini!" he was yelling. Could it be? Mirette's heart hammered in her chest.

Bellini stepped out onto the wire and saluted the crowd. He took a step and then froze. The crowd cheered wildly. But something was wrong. Mirette knew at once what it was. For a moment she was as frozen as Bellini was.

Then she threw herself at the door behind her, ran inside, up flight after flight of stairs, and out through a skylight to the roof.

She stretched her hands to Bellini. He smiled and began to walk toward her. She stepped onto the wire, and with the most intense pleasure, as she had always imagined it might be, she started to cross the sky.

"Brava! Bravo!" roared the crowd.

"Protégée of the Great Bellini!" shouted the agent. He was beside himself, already planning the world tour of Bellini and Mirette.

As for the master and his pupil, they were thinking only of the wire, and of crossing to the end.

ABOUT THE AUTHOR
EMILY ARNOLD MCCULLY

Emily Arnold McCully has written and illustrated many picture books, including the award-winning *Picnic*, and her artwork has been displayed internationally. She also writes for adults. Her book *A Craving* was nominated for an American Book Award.

Balancing Act

The Toronto Star,
August 27, 1996

Circus life has its ups and downs for a young performer who loves the excitement but craves a friend.

By Al Sokol
STAFF REPORTER

Audrey Brisson-Jutras wants a friend.

"It doesn't matter if it's a girl or boy. I would prefer a girl, but a boy would be okay, too," she offers.

The lack of a friend—a real friend who can do the stuff eleven-year-olds like to do—is a drawback of circus life for the young performer in Cirque du Soleil.

And with three years on the road living in a trailer ahead of her, she's not likely to get her wish anytime soon.

But Audrey, who plays a starring role in Cirque's newest production, *Quidam*, is quick to point out the upside of her unconventional lifestyle.

"This is a wonderful experience. I get to work with a lot of different and very talented people. We're like family here. We look after each other.

"I don't think I'm missing out on anything by being in the show, but I would like someone my age to play with or just talk to," she adds, a trifle wistfully.

"Sometimes I wonder if other people think I'm just a little kid and don't take me seriously.

"So, sure. I would like another eleven-year-old kid to be here."

Here is under the big top, a 2500-seat blue and yellow tent set up at Ontario Place. The show is there until September 8 when it leaves for Santa Monica, California, the next stop on a thirteen-city North American tour that will add up to more than a thousand performances before a potential 2.5 million people.

It will be the fall of 1998 before Audrey returns for good to her hometown of Montreal, where *Quidam* (pronounced kee-dam), opened last April.

Until then, she can only make short visits periodically to see her mother, opera singer Martine Brisson, who is her vocal coach, and

"This is a wonderful experience. I get to work with a lot of different and very talented people. We're like family here. We look after each other."

four-year-old stepbrother.

Her father, Benoît Jutras, who composed *Quidam*'s powerful music, travels with Audrey in the show.

Audrey says she has never taken any formal voice training but between her mother and father, "I should be able to sing."

Her character is the essence of *Quidam*, a magic mixture of music, Greek tragedy, and Olympic Games gymnastics. She wanders the stage lamenting, in song, that she has seen everything there is to see and her world has lost all meaning.

(Cirque du Soleil, which began as a small show in Montreal twelve years ago, uses only humans—no animals.)

Audrey and her husky, haunting voice are front and centre for most of the two hours of high-voltage creativity.

There are many nights, she says, when she doesn't get to sleep until 1:00 a.m. because she is too wound up after an evening's performance.

Sometimes 10:30 a.m. is too early for school to start, she complains mildly. Audrey and six other Cirque youngsters ranging in age from six to sixteen must attend classes five days a week in a nearby trailer supervised by teachers Sabine Cyr, thirty, and Jean Gelineau, thirty-three. (Four young Chinese girls, who turn a child's game of Oriental yo-yos into high entertainment, go to another school supervised by their chaperone from Beijing.)

Audrey and fellow performer Olga Pikhienko hit the books with teacher Jean Gelineau.

Audrey appears in *Quidam*'s nine performances a week. Monday is the only day off but on those days she flies back to Montreal to complete the vocals for the show's CD, expected to be released this fall.

She gets a bit of a break between cities because it takes a week to put up the 2500-seat tent, which includes an amazing thirty-six-metre overhead conveyor system, and three days to get it down.

The travelling show, featuring more than fifty performers from such countries as Canada, Russia, China, United States, Austria, France, and Switzerland, has its own hydro, kitchen, air conditioning, and school. All it needs to be in business is a fire hydrant on the site.

The pace and demands of the show haven't diminished Audrey's enthusiasm. She actually got her first taste of circus life as a four-year-old when she performed on a balance bicycle for one season.

"I retired after the bicycle act until this year when my father was asked if I would be interested in being a performer," she explains.

Now, she has a three-year contract "but I'd like to stay with the show for six.

"I was a little nervous when *Quidam* opened in Montreal. Now that's over. I like to be on stage and that's the truth."

No Ordinary Baby:

Wolfgang Amadeus Mozart

Born in Salzburg, Austria, 1756
Died in Vienna, Austria, 1791
Austrian composer who in his short life wrote
many masterpieces, including symphonies, operas
such as The Magic Flute *and* Don Giovanni,
and piano music

by Kathleen Krull
Illustrated by Eric Colquhoun

Until he was three, Wolfgang Amadeus Mozart was an ordinary baby.

Then he began climbing up on the bench and imitating the clavier playing of his talented older sister Maria Anna. At age four, he made up his own compositions and studied violin. He insisted that all his activities be accompanied by music. His father noticed that it was difficult to teach him music—he seemed to know everything already. By the time he was five, he would stay up late, practising by candlelight.

The next year, six-year-old Mozart went on tour, travelling by stagecoach all around the bumpy roads of Europe. (From all of his travels, Mozart eventually learned to speak fifteen languages.) He played for royalty, for the well-known musicians of the day, and in bars. At seven, he proposed marriage to Marie Antoinette (the future queen of France); at eight, he was composing symphonies; and at eleven, he composed his first opera. When composing, Mozart wore an apron to keep the ink off his clothes. He wore little velvet coats with lace ruffles and gold embroidery, and a little gold sword at his side.

He was known then as the most-kissed little boy in Europe. Today we think of him as the greatest musical prodigy who ever lived.

Mozart had a strange and exhausting childhood. He was so often ill that some people worried about how much longer he would live. He was sweet and affectionate, most anxious to please. His special talent meant he never had to go to school; his father gave him lessons. Mozart especially liked arithmetic and covered tablecloths and wallpaper with rows of figures.

Mozart loved animals. He sent the family dog, a terrier named Bimperl, greetings from cities all over Europe. In London, he broke off a concert to run after a cat that had wandered in. Later in life, he owned two other dogs (Goukerl and Katherl), a pet grasshopper, and various birds.

As a child Mozart was cute, with rosy cheeks and bright eyes. As an adult, though, his skin was yellowish, scarred from smallpox, and his blue eyes were bulgy. He was short and thin, and his head was too big for his body. Yet he was concerned about his appearance. He took care to have elegant clothes, and he had a barber work on his hair much more often than most people did.

Mozart fell madly in love with

Aloysia Weber (cousin of composer Carl Maria von Weber), his landlady's daughter. But she rejected him, and he married Constanze Weber, her sister. Constanze was like Mozart in many ways: musical, not especially attractive (he called her "Little Mouse"), and playful. They had six children, but only two lived to adulthood.

Music was the one thing that made Mozart's face light up. He usually woke up at six, composed till nine, gave music lessons till one (though he didn't enjoy teaching), then had lunch at someone's house, where he had to entertain his hosts. Then, unless there was a concert to attend, he composed far into the night. He could get by on as little as four hours' sleep. Doctors told him he needed to get more regular recreation, which may be why he eventually bought a pool table.

He wrote music more quickly than almost any other composer in history, and he sometimes put things off till the very last minute. If he had to work through the night, Constanze would tell him tales about Cinderella or Aladdin to keep him awake.

His best ideas came when he was in a good mood, alone, and undisturbed. "What a delight this is I cannot tell!" he once wrote. "All this inventing, this producing, takes place in a pleasing, lively dream."

He could write down his ideas at meals (he liked liver dumplings and sauerkraut), while gossiping with friends, and even while playing pool. Once he held his wife's hand during childbirth and with his other hand wrote several pieces of music.

One day a visitor found Mozart and his wife dancing in their house, and Mozart explained that they had run out of firewood and were trying to stay warm. Mozart spent money faster than he could earn it, and he was always in debt. Part of the problem was that aristocrats paid him for music with things like watches and snuff boxes—not the cash that he needed to live on. (A letter that he wrote asking for a loan sold, two centuries later, for one hundred times the amount he had pleaded for.)

There were plenty of people who didn't like Mozart. They thought he was rude, immature, and irresponsible. One person who knew Mozart well said that she never heard him say one serious thing. He could be impatient with people who were not as bright as he was.

Although his father was always bombarding him with advice on how to make money and meet the "right" people, Mozart had trouble finding and keeping jobs. Once he lost a court appointment by being obnoxious and got himself literally kicked out of court. "There is the door; I will have nothing more to do with such a villain," said the man who fired him.

Mozart was scared of ghosts and loud noises, and he was superstitious, which explains his reaction to the tall, mysterious stranger who came to his house one night. Dressed all in grey, the stranger commissioned him to write a requiem (or funeral) mass.

The stranger would never give his name, but kept nagging Mozart to finish. Fearful, and convinced somehow that he was writing his *own* burial music, Mozart worked feverishly. Eventually the stranger was revealed to be a messenger from an eccentric count who had a habit of having well-known composers write something he could pass off as his own in private performances.

But by that time Mozart had died of kidney failure and malnutrition.

Mozart had spent fourteen years of his short life on the road, and he had never been very healthy. He was only thirty-five when he died. Some people feel that fear of the stranger hastened his death. Plays, operas, and movies have been written about the theory that he was poisoned by rival composer Antonio Salieri, but this rumor has never been proved.

At the peak of his career, Mozart earned as much money in one concert as his father earned in a year. Yet, at the time of his death, he owned very little. He had six coats (five red, his favorite color, and one white for court); three silver spoons; and 346 books. His most expensive possessions were his walnut piano and his pool table.

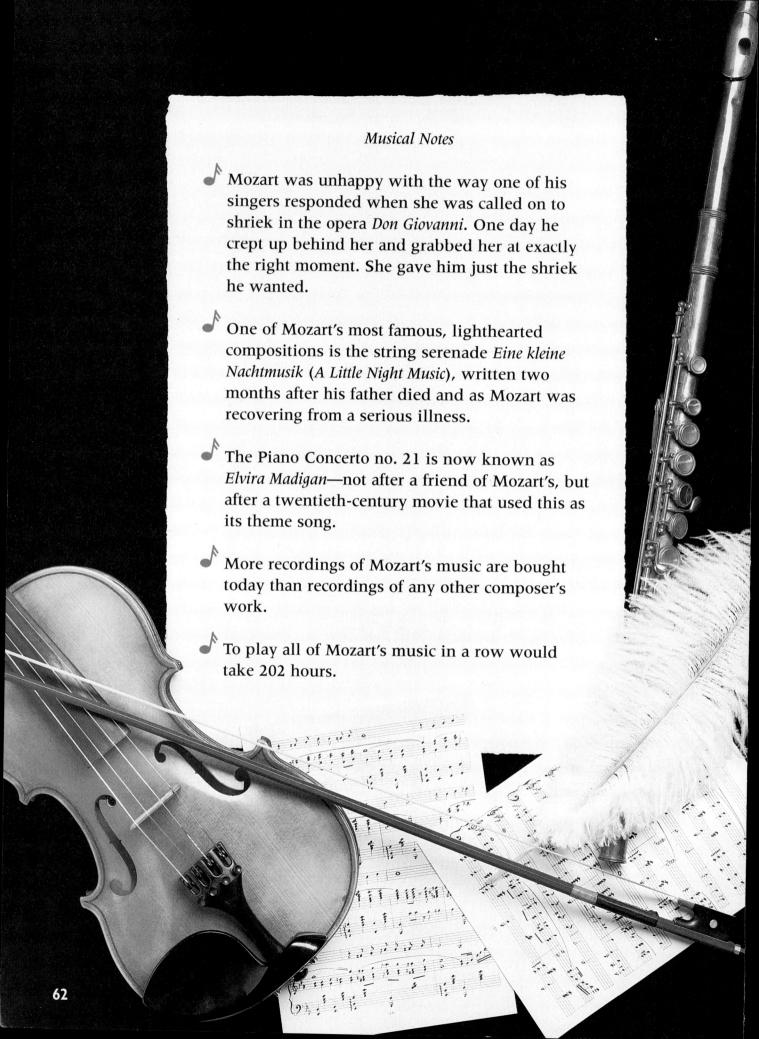

Musical Notes

♪ Mozart was unhappy with the way one of his singers responded when she was called on to shriek in the opera *Don Giovanni*. One day he crept up behind her and grabbed her at exactly the right moment. She gave him just the shriek he wanted.

♪ One of Mozart's most famous, lighthearted compositions is the string serenade *Eine kleine Nachtmusik* (*A Little Night Music*), written two months after his father died and as Mozart was recovering from a serious illness.

♪ The Piano Concerto no. 21 is now known as *Elvira Madigan*—not after a friend of Mozart's, but after a twentieth-century movie that used this as its theme song.

♪ More recordings of Mozart's music are bought today than recordings of any other composer's work.

♪ To play all of Mozart's music in a row would take 202 hours.

Nervous Singing

Sally was sweating all over as she was next in turn for the audition of the part of Cinderella. She had been rehearsing all night and woke up with a sore throat, and feared that her voice would come out repulsive for her singing part.

As somebody shoved her onto the stage, she froze with stage fright. She then began to sing:

"Sooo this is love," she croaked in a terrible voice. She took a deep breath, hoping for the best, and tried again:

"Sooo this is love, my handsome prince . . ." she finished with a beautiful voice.

"Bravo!" a skinny man yelled, "you have the part!"

Sally smiled gleefully, as her hard work had paid off!

Nelly Nashid
Age 12

The Chinese Youth Goodwill Mission

On October 2, the Chinese Youth Goodwill Mission presented one hour of adventure in Chinese dances, songs, kung fu, and folk arts in the University of Waterloo's Humanities Theatre. This opened our eyes to Taiwan's fascinating culture. Part of what made it so fascinating were the brightly colored ribbons and costumes. It also taught me a little about the history of Taiwan, my homeland. Eighteen dedicated and spirited dancers danced with all their energy, so you could not help but love the performance. I recommend that all who love culture see this show the next time it comes to their community.

Florence Ting
Grade 6

Student Writing

The Circus Performer

Once there was this really cool clown. Everyone thought he was the best. "Look, there he is!" one of the kids in the crowd said.

"Hello, everybody!" the clown said in the microphone. Then he started performing. He was riding a little bike, then he stopped. He pulled a little box out of his pocket. Then he pressed a button on it. "Wow, cool!" a kid yelled. It turned into an Indy car. He started to race around the stage. The car roared. Then the clown lost control of the car. "Aahh!" he screamed. Crash!!! The car got all smashed up. "Are you okay?" the fire breather said with smoke coming out of his mouth.

"He's fine, he's fine," remarked the clown's boss. "I'm mad at you, you clown," yelled the mad boss.

"Oh-oh, you're in big trouble," insisted the fire breather.

"Come in my office in ten minutes," ordered the boss again. The clown went into the office. He opened the door.

"Congratulations!" said the boss.

"What?" questioned the clown.

"Everyone loved you out there! Let's do that again!" said the boss.

"Huh?!" said the confused clown.

Daniel Gunton
Age 11

For me, writing is hard to start, but I get carried away once I have written a few paragraphs. It is easier to write about things that have happened, because then I know how to describe how the person is feeling, or about the situation.

Florence Ting

Behind the Scenes

by Amanda Lewis and
Tim Wynne -Jones
Illustrated by Renée Mansfield

PROPS

The props department has to find or make all the things that the actors need on stage. Props must be easy to use, lightweight, and durable. A special machine called a Vacuform can make plastic copies of all sorts of detailed shapes, from jewellery to a roast pig. If a play needs soldiers outfitted in armor, the props people make a breastplate mould of modelling clay. It can be used in the Vacuform machine to create as many plastic copies as required. When the plastic has cooled, it can be painted to look like solid steel or decorated with fake gems. The plastic is hard and strong, and makes a satisfying *thunk* when hit with a prop sword.

Imagine a merchant in an old-fashioned market. He appears to be carrying a live chicken in a crate. During every performance, right on cue, the chicken has to squawk and crash around inside the crate. How would you make such a prop?

The prop designer wound up a wooden stick with elastic bands (like a propeller), put it in a crate filled with feathers, and held it in place with a latch. When the actor released the latch, the stick twirled and clattered against the crate and feathers flew out between the slats. Instant chicken!

Props—even fake chickens—are set out on a table backstage before each show, and must be returned so they can be found when needed.

Sometimes a prop will have to change in appearance during the play. An umbrella that looks fine in act 1 may have to look ripped apart in act 4. A purse may have to be covered in mud in one scene and clean by the next. The props people will get two identical umbrellas and rip one up. They'll get two identical purses and slap mud all over one. Both umbrellas and purses will sit on the props table so the actors can take the right one on stage for each scene.

The people in props need to know how to sew, glue, paint, carve, mould, and how to be very inventive!

COSTUME DESIGNER

The costume designer works with the director to create a special look for each character. Each costume reveals facts about the character's social position, personality, tastes, and habits. But whether a character is rich or poor, showy or sloppy, all the costumes for all the characters must go together. In this way, the costume designer creates a look for the whole play.

The costume designer makes a sketch of each actor as his or her character. These sketches are based on information in the play and on the director's ideas about that character. The designer creates a sketch for each change of clothing the character needs and chooses the fabrics to use.

The actor's measurements, a description of every costume, and swatches of the fabrics are given to the cutters and sewers in the costume department, and they transform the sketch into reality.

SET DESIGNER

The set designer must work closely with the director to establish the period and style of the play. This might involve research into how a particular group of people lived in a certain time and place. Shakespeare's play *The Tempest* starts with a scene of a ship in a storm. But what kind of ship: an ancient galleon, a royal yacht, a cruise ship? The set is often the first thing that the audience sees. It lets the audience know where and when in history the play takes place. It tells part of the story.

The set can be elaborate and detailed or it can merely suggest a location: one or two trees can stand for a whole forest; a bed and lamp can be a bedroom; a bale of hay and a pitchfork, a barn; a large box and two flashlights, a car. A set can be realistic or fanciful; imagine a dining room where the table, chairs, carpet, and sideboard are all striped like a zebra!

Because a set often has to be changed from scene to scene, sets must look solid but actually be light and easy to move. Often large structures—walls, rocks, archways—have to be moved in less than a minute. A huge sailing vessel may have to be replaced by a courtyard as the audience waits and watches. Sets must be designed to be put together and taken apart with ease and efficiency.

The set designer must have the skills of an architect, an interior designer, a historian, a sculptor, and a painter. She or he must also know everything that happens in the play. For example, if an actor is to climb up to a balcony, sturdy footholds must be built into the set. And if a character is to look out a window, there must *be* a window to look out or someone is going to feel very foolish!

STAGE MANAGER

The stage manager is the person who has to know what everyone else is doing. She or he has to be able to answer everyone's questions and solve everyone's problems. A lot of people work together to put on a show–in costumes, lighting, sound, props, sets, make-up, front of house–and the stage manager must make sure that all of them know what they're supposed to be doing.

The stage manager also organizes rehearsals so that all the actors are there when they are needed. During rehearsals, the stage manager must make notes of all the director's decisions—the blocking (where the actors move and when); when lights come on; when a sound cue happens; changes in costumes, props, or sets ("That wall should be blue, not green"); everything that needs fixing or that hasn't been done yet.

A prompt book contains all the information about the actual running of the play. It might be a three-ring binder or scrapbook. On one page is a page from the play. Across from it might be an outline of the stage, on which the stage manager draws little arrows to show where the actor is to move. Beside each arrow a number indicates when in the play the actor is supposed to go there. If an actor forgets his or her moves or lines, the stage manager can find them in the book. Other numbers are used to remind the stage manager of the sound and light cues. During the actual run of the show, the stage manager can make sure that the sounds and lights happen when they are supposed to.

You can read a stage manager's prompt book and, with a little imagination, see and hear the whole play in your mind's eye.

LIGHTING

Lighting, like sets and costumes, is specifically designed for each show. But good lighting seems invisible—it's only when something goes wrong that the audience notices. Imagine an actor in the centre of the stage speaking in total darkness while across from him, the stairs are brightly lit! Proper light helps the audience to focus on what is important to see. It also helps to create the mood of a scene.

Lights of many sizes and shapes are used to create different effects on stage. They are all carefully hung on metal bars high above the stage and aimed at specific places on the stage. "Gels," thin pieces of colored plastic, are put in front of the bulbs to change the color of the light. A scene bathed in pale blue light will seem cold and forbidding. The same scene bathed in orange will look warm and inviting.

The lighting designer and the director decide when certain lights should come on and how bright each should be. The lighting technician then programs these lighting cues into a computerized lighting system so that the lights will come on at their proper level at the push of a button.

The technician can see the stage from the lighting booth and can talk through an intercom with the stage manager, who says when to begin a lighting cue and thus change the lighting on the stage.

SOUND

Today, theatres use both live and recorded sounds. Recordings can be played through speakers throughout the theatre so that the sound comes from all around, or, played from one speaker to another, the sound can seem to be travelling.

Recordings of some sounds can be borrowed from sound libraries, then changed to go faster or slower, louder or softer, as needed.

If there is supposed to be a large crowd fighting off-stage, the sound engineer can record a few people making the right noises. Then that can be re-recorded and layered over and over to make it seem like a large, noisy crowd.

The sound designer and the director decide how loud and long each sound effect should be. These sound cues are then programmed into a computer so that the sound operator can play them at appropriate moments during the show.

THE DIRECTOR

The director of a play is like an orchestra conductor. His or her first job is to read the play through many times to find what is special or interesting about it. The director must make the point of the play clear and the relationships between the characters easy to understand. Each director will see a play differently. Each will find different things in the words and actions that are important.

The director usually decides which actors should play which parts. Then the director and the designers decide what period, style, and mood the play will be in. All the words, actors, costumes, props, sets, make-up, light, and sound must work together so that the world they create on stage makes sense.

The Leopard's Noisy Drum

by Janice Kuharski
Photographed by Gilbert Duclos

CHARACTERS

Nyame, *the sky god*
Elephant
Lion
Bear
Turtle
Leopard

SCENE I

TIME: *Long ago.*

SETTING: *Tropical forest in western Africa. Tall stool is centre.*

AT RISE: *Sound of rhythmic drumbeats is heard off-stage. NYAME, carrying staff, enters and sits on stool.*

NYAME (*Yelling over sound of drum and pounding ground with staff*): Where is everyone? I called a meeting over an hour ago! (LION *and* BEAR *rush on.*)

LION: Good morning, Nyame. Sorry we're late.

BEAR: I was nearly caught in a trap. Thank goodness Lion came along when he did! (*They sit on floor, centre right, facing NYAME. ELEPHANT rushes on, followed by TURTLE, who moves slowly.*)

ELEPHANT: Am I late? Did I miss anything? (*Sits*)

NYAME (*Shouting over drum, which gradually fades out*): Something must be done about Leopard's noisy drum! (TURTLE *finally reaches centre and sits.*) The drum keeps everyone in the forest awake, and what's worse, everyone complains to me about it. How can I work on a rainstorm when my time is taken up with silly complaints?

LION (*Apologetically*): But, Your Majesty, we've already tried to steal the drum and we've had no luck.

NYAME (*Pounding staff angrily*): Then you must try again! All of you together will go this evening at sunset.

BEAR (*Quickly*): I—I'm afraid I can't go this time. I've got a terrible stomach ache. (*Holds stomach and groans*) Until my stomach is better, I couldn't possibly go on a long trip through the forest.

NYAME: Very well. If Bear cannot go, then Lion and Elephant will go.

LION: Unfortunately, Your Majesty, I can't go either—at least not until my paw has healed. (LION *holds up front paw.*) I stepped on a huge thorn and walking even a short distance is terribly painful. (*Puts paw to ground and winces*)

NYAME (*Poking* ELEPHANT *with his staff*): Then Elephant must go alone. After all, he is bigger and stronger than either Lion or Bear.

ELEPHANT (*Stands, takes a step back*): I, Your Majesty? Go alone—by myself? (*Backing toward exit*) I'm afraid I can't go. Without company, I'd probably fall asleep. Leopard's noisy drum kept me awake all last night. (*Yawns loudly*) In fact, I must go take a nap right now.

NYAME (*Bellowing*): Forget the nap, Elephant! (ELEPHANT *jumps, startled.*) Get back here at once.

ELEPHANT (*Quickly returning and sitting down*): Yes, Your Majesty.

NYAME (*In commanding voice*): I am the sky god! I have things to take care of—thunder, lightning, rainbow, et cetera, et cetera. And if I don't get back to work soon, the rain forest will have no rain. (*Pounds staff on ground; firmly*) One of you must go—and that is final.

BEAR (*Matter-of-factly*): I was the first to go last time. This time, either Lion or Elephant should go first.

LION: Excuse me, Bear, but *I* was the first to go last time.

ELEPHANT (*Indignantly*): You both have short memories. I went first. Then Bear went, and Lion went last.

NYAME (*Waving staff at them; angrily*) Stop this ridiculous quarrel! I'm tired of excuses. (*Bellows*) Bring me the drum—now!

LION (*Cowering*): Your Majesty, if I may suggest—

TURTLE (*Inching closer to* NYAME): Excuse me for interrupting, Nyame, but I think I have a solution to everyone's problem. I will go get the drum.

BEAR, ELEPHANT, *and* **LION** (*Amused; ad lib*): What? You're joking! No way! (*Etc.*)

ELEPHANT: If *we* couldn't get Leopard's noisy drum—and we're a hundred times stronger and faster than you—how could you possibly get the drum?

LION (*Boasting*): I'd say we're a *thousand* times faster and stronger! Maybe a million times—

NYAME (*Shouting and pounding staff*): Silence! (LION *trembles.*) It's Turtle's turn to speak. (*Kindly*) Well, Turtle, what is your plan?

TURTLE: It's true that Elephant, Lion, and Bear could not steal Leopard's drum, but that's because he was expecting them. He would not be expecting me.

NYAME (*Stroking chin and nodding*): An excellent point! But even if you do catch Leopard off guard, how do you plan to steal the drum?

BEAR (*Skeptically*): You couldn't even *lift* the drum!

ELEPHANT (*Haughtily*): It's *much* too big and heavy for you.

TURTLE: If my plan works, my part of the task will be easy. Leopard will do the hard part—all by himself!

NYAME: Well, then, it's settled. Turtle will steal the drum.

TURTLE: Thank you, Nyame. (*Turning and starting slowly toward exit*) I will leave now to get a head start.

OTHERS (*Waving to* TURTLE; *ad lib*): Goodbye, Turtle. Good luck. (*Etc. Curtain.*)

Scene II

TIME: *One month later.*

SETTING: *Deep in the forest. Tall stool is centre; shorter stool is left.*

AT RISE: LEOPARD *is seated on tall stool, beating drum.* TURTLE *enters left and slowly moves to centre and sits on smaller stool.*

LEOPARD (*Pounding drum and chanting*):

> The forest is mine
> all night and all day.
> The sound of my drum
> keeps others away.
>
> Let the Lion or Bear
> or the Elephant come;
> each one of them fears
> the sound of my drum.
>
> My music is magic;
> my singing is grand.
> While I have a drum,
> I'm ruler of the land.

TURTLE (*Shouting over drum*): Good morning, Leopard. I've been listening to your music. You have a fine-sounding drum and a fine voice as well. (LEOPARD *stops pounding drum and looks up.*)

LEOPARD (*Flattered*): Why, thank you, Turtle. (*Boasting*) I do have the best and biggest drum in the forest.

TURTLE: Without a doubt, you have the best-sounding drum I've ever heard—but not the biggest.

LEOPARD (*Irritated; stepping down from stool*): How can you say that? There is no drum in the forest bigger than mine!

TURTLE: That would be true—if the great Nyame did not have an even bigger drum.

LEOPARD: Impossible! No drum is bigger than this. (TURTLE *gets up and inspects drum.*)

TURTLE: It's a fine drum, indeed. But Nyame's drum is so large that he can fit inside his—with room to spare! Can you do the same?

LEOPARD (*Quickly*): Of course I can! (*Considering*) I mean, I'm sure I could if I tried.

TURTLE (*Shaking his head*): No, I don't think you could fit in this drum. (*Smugly*) I don't think this drum is even half as big as Nyame's. (TURTLE *sits again.*)

LEOPARD (*Upset*): If Nyame can fit inside his drum, then I can fit inside my drum as well.

TURTLE: I've *seen* Nyame get inside his drum.

LEOPARD (*Hotly*): Then you shall see me get inside my drum, as well! (*Puts drum on its side.*) But you will need to tell me when I am completely inside. (*Begins to crawl into drum headfirst*)

TURTLE (*Going to drum*): It would be a great honor.

LEOPARD (*Wiggling forward inside drum*): How am I doing, Turtle?

TURTLE: Your hindquarters are still showing, Leopard.

LEOPARD (*Inching forward*): Am I inside the drum yet, Turtle?

TURTLE (*Smiling broadly*): Almost, but your tail is still showing.

LEOPARD (*Pulling tail inside drum*): I can't see a thing—it's dark in here. Can you see me now?

TURTLE: Not even a speck of you is showing now.

LEOPARD (*Panicked*): Help me, Turtle. I'm stuck. I can't turn around in here. Get me out!

TURTLE: I will let you out, Leopard, but not until I've brought you to Nyame. (*Aside*) Thank goodness much of the way home is downhill this time. Leopard's drum should roll nicely—all the way home.

LEOPARD (*Pounding frantically*): Let me out! Let me out or you'll be sorry, Turtle!

TURTLE: My advice to you, Leopard, is to stop complaining and make yourself comfortable. You'll have plenty of time for a nice long nap. (*Curtain*)

SCENE III

SETTING: *Same as Scene I. Tall stool is centre.*

AT RISE: NYAME *sits on stool. ELEPHANT, BEAR, and LION sit on floor. TURTLE stands next to drum, centre left. Sounds of banging and pounding from inside drum are heard intermittently.*

ELEPHANT: It's been so long since you left, Turtle. We didn't think you were coming back.

TURTLE (*Proudly*): I am not only back, but I have the drum as well.

NYAME: How were you able to bring Leopard's drum back all by yourself?

TURTLE: That was easy. Many animals in the forest wanted to get a closer look at Leopard's wonderful drum. So they were only too happy to help me push.

NYAME (*Admiringly*): Ah! A very clever plan, indeed, my friend!

LEOPARD (*From inside drum; furious*): Let me out! Let me out!

NYAME: What is that horrible racket?

TURTLE: It's Leopard, and except for when he's sleeping, he's been screaming like that since we started out. What shall I do with him, Nyame?

ELEPHANT: The only thing you can do, Nyame, is banish Leopard from the forest.

LION (*Eagerly*): Yes, yes. Banish him—and the sooner the better! (*Boastfully*) Then I will be the undisputed ruler of the forest.

BEAR (*Scornfully*): That's not true, Lion. I should be the one to rule the forest, not you.

ELEPHANT: *I* should be the ruler of the forest. After all, I'm the tallest, the heaviest, and the strongest.

TURTLE: Your Majesty, I have a suggestion. If Leopard is not around, these three will never agree on who should be ruler of the forest. And the noise from their endless squabbling will be even worse than the sound of Leopard's drum.

NYAME (*Gets down from stool and paces; stroking his chin*): An excellent point, Turtle. I could not stand another commotion. Leopard is free to return to his home in the forest. (ELEPHANT *helps* LEOPARD *climb out of drum.*)

LEOPARD (*Shaking himself out; indignantly*): It's about time! (*Fluffing himself*) Look! My fur is all matted! (*Grumbling as he exits*) I'm still ruler of the forest, you know!

TURTLE (*Gestures toward drum*): And here is the drum you asked for, Nyame. What will you do with it?

NYAME (*Setting drum upright*): Leopard's drum is just what I need to make loud rolls of thunder. Listen! (NYAME *beats drum, as thunder is heard off-stage.* ELEPHANT, BEAR, *and* LION *cower and cover ears.* NYAME *turns toward* TURTLE, *pleased.*) You have done what Elephant, Bear, and Lion could not do. What reward shall I give you?

TURTLE (*Thinking*): Well . . . I have always wanted a house that I could carry on my back when I travel.

NYAME (*Nods*): A fine idea! That is exactly what you shall have. (*Exits and returns carrying shell; ties shell on* TURTLE's *back*)

ELEPHANT (*Walking around* TURTLE, *inspecting shell*): It's magnificent! Look at the colors—olive green and yellow, even a bit of red.

BEAR (*Looking at shell*): And it has a nice design around the edge.

LION (*Nodding*): The shape fits his body perfectly.

ELEPHANT (*Thinking*): I could use something like that—only bigger, of course.

BEAR: How ridiculous! You don't need a shell. But I could certainly use one.

LION: And so could I. (*Eagerly*) Let's ask Nyame. (*Turns toward* NYAME) Your Majesty, do you think each of us could have a shell just like Turtle's?

NYAME (*Stroking chin*): Perhaps we should ask Turtle what he thinks of your request. (*Turns to* TURTLE) Well, Turtle, what do you say?

TURTLE: I think that if Lion, Elephant, and Bear each had a shell, they would be even stronger than they already are. It would not be fair to give them shells . . . unless each one agrees to give up something that makes him strong.

NYAME: I see your point. What do you think a fair exchange would be?

BEAR, ELEPHANT, *and* **LION** (*Excitedly*): Yes, tell us! (*Each in turn looks taken aback as* TURTLE *speaks.*)

TURTLE: Well, Elephant could give up his strong tusks. Lion could give up his strong teeth, and Bear could give up his mighty claws.

NYAME (*Pounding staff*): A splendid idea! Shells in exchange for tusks, teeth, and claws. I'll do it at once!

BEAR, ELEPHANT, *and* **LION** (*Ad lib; alarmed*): No! Wait! We can't do that!

ELEPHANT: I really don't need a shell after all!

LION: Nor do I. A shell would cover my beautiful mane.

BEAR: I don't need one either. A heavy shell would just slow me down.

NYAME (*Firmly*): Then stop wasting my time with your foolishness! I have work to do! (NYAME *beats drum, and thunder is heard off.*) A rain forest must have rain, you know! Now that I have Leopard's drum, I'll shake the skies open and *let the rain come!* (*Lights dim. Thunder is heard and lights flash.* BEAR, LION, *and* ELEPHANT *cower and cover ears.* TURTLE *pulls head under shell and moves toward exit. Curtain closes.*)

THE END

Production Notes

THE LEOPARD'S NOISY DRUM

Characters: 6 male or female

Playing time: 20 minutes

Costumes: Nyame wears grey beard, colorful African robe and hat, sandals. Appropriate animal costumes: Elephant has tusks and trunk; Bear has claws; Lion has large teeth; and Leopard has spotted coat. Turtle wears green body stocking. All wear face paint.

Properties: Tall drum painted with colorful African design. Must be large enough for Leopard to crawl inside. Staff or walking stick. Large papier-mâché turtle shell that can be tied onto Turtle.

Setting: Forest. Backdrop depicts tall trees, vines, monkeys, colorful birds, snakes, etc. Tall stool is centre in Scenes I and III. Second, shorter stool is next to it in Scene II.

Sound: Recorded African drum music; thunder.

Lighting: Lights dim at the end of the play, followed by flashes of lighting.

*Note: In the original text, the creatures are all male. However the characters may be portrayed by either males or females.

When Will I Be Good Enough?

I waited for this moment.
Practised every line.
Rehearsed every gesture
My tone just right.
Felt so confident.
Am I good enough?

Entered the room boldly.
Acknowledged the judges.
My heart pounding.
My stomach tied in knots.

Control, control.
Take deep breaths.
I do not recognize my voice.
Why do I tremble so?

"Thank you. You may leave.
We'll call you."
The words fade as I exit.
Do I dare try again?
Was I good enough?

Jermaine Griffin
Age 12

I really enjoy writing a lot. Writing on this theme made me enjoy it even more. I, too, was once in a play. It was called "Joseph and the Amazing Technicolor Dreamcoat." Although I had few lines, it felt great speaking in front of a large audience.

Jermaine Griffin

Putting on a Play

This story began when a little wee lad from Canada wanted to play the role of Peter Pan in the school production. It seemed as though everyone wanted to play this part. Now this little boy's name was John Travolta. John was Peter Pan's biggest fan. When the time came for auditions, John was no doubt the best at playing Peter Pan. He got the job on the spot. "All right!" he said with joy. "As soon as I get my lines I'm going to learn them." And with that he ran home very excited. Within the next few days he had his lines memorized perfectly. On the night of the production, John was the only one who spoke like he was just speaking naturally. Someone in the audience noticed this. She spread the word and now you will find him on TV.

Katherine Corney
Age 11